FRAGMENTS
OF
PREHISTORIC WISDOM

Translated Teachings of a Lost Civilization

R.C. & Team

CONTEXT

In 2019, during routine excavation on private land I own in an undisclosed region, my team and I uncovered what may be one of the most significant archaeological discoveries of our time: a cache of artifacts, including over 400 stone tablets bearing inscriptions unlike any known script. These mostly literary artifacts defy conventional dating methods but are estimated—based on stratigraphy and material composition—to predate the earliest known written texts, including cuneiform, and even what we've long considered the earliest established civilizations. The implications are staggering. In fact, the very concept of "history" begins to seem juvenile.

The language, wholly unique, does not appear to share any discernible lineage with any known linguistic family. Yet, through exhaustive analysis of the patterns, syntax, and symbolic relationships within the inscriptions, my team—through painstaking, scholarly efforts—has managed to assemble this tentative translation. The process has been fraught with uncertainty, as we have had no way to confirm its accuracy. Instead, we have relied on the internal consistency of the texts themselves, gradually piecing together fragments of meaning over the past five years.

Thus, while this represents the only coherent reconstruction to date, the resulting work you hold is an imperfect and incomplete translation. We have relied on a combination of contextual clues, symbolism, and comparative analysis. Some analects proved impossible to translate, and many remain undeciphered. We cannot be certain that we've presented them in any logical, meaningful, or correct order. The exact nature of these people remains a mystery. While we struggle to discern the structure of their analects, the pervasive sense of urgency and profound depth of thought that does reach us is unmistakable. Not aligning with our understanding of any known civilization at the time, we cannot confidently hypothesize where this society fits within the broader timeline of human development. Despite all this, these ideas etched into stone resonate with timeless relevance, as though the authors are speaking directly to distant posterity; directly to us.

Each fragment corresponds to an individual stone tablet, with variations in inscription size, depth, and clarity. The stones themselves were degraded to such an extent that direct preservation or reproduction of the script has proved impossible. We have photographed the specimens from every possible angle and intend to make the exhibition public in due course. Until then, their location shall remain undisclosed, as the site must be protected from interference, insidious intentions, and political sabotage, while research continues.

I present this text because we are all in this together. Everything we think we know is now in question. If 'primitive' people saw the human story as a cycle, and 'civilized' people view it as a straight line with a beginning, middle, and end… then *we* must now see it as an open field to wander freely, for history is broken —————— go!

——— RC & team

TRANSLATIONS

1.

Thanks to the Mighty Spirit

from which all is made

and which fills every pore of the universe.

2.

Everything we see proceeds from this

original, thinking, formless substance.

3.

There is no limit in the supply

of the infinite Mighty Spirit.

4.

[Unreadable due to damage]

5.

The desire you feel for more, more, more,

is the infinite itself seeking expression through you.

6.

Your role is to express this desire back.

7.

The Mighty Spirit desires

those who can play music

to have instruments for playing.

8.

Our duty is to cultivate

our talents to the fullest extent.

9.

To do your duty without

asking for favors in return

is to become like the rain:

what can the world do

in return for the rain?

10.

Discover thy work, and do it.

11.

The stone knows its shape

before the hammer strikes;

the stars do not wait

for the night to call.

12.

The silence is louder than the roar.

13.

Roots are hidden, [unreadable due to damage]
Strength of the tree.

14.

Eye-sight is in conflict with inner-knowing.

15.

Strive hard as we may,

what we don't deserve

doesn't stay… and

what we deserve,

we cannot dispose of.

16.

Why bemoan the gifts of misery,

when you enjoy the gifts of pleasure

without complaint?

17.

Any rodent can hoard material wealth,

the gains of compassion are most precious.

18.

To seek the end is to chase a shadow,

to chase the beginning is to masturbate.

19

Fire is not born of wood, nor is wood born of fire.

Fire is the breath of wood. Wood is the form of fire.

20

The hunter is not the one who chases the beast.

The hunter is the one who waits, and,

in waiting, becomes the beast.

21.

There is no direction until you walk.

22.

Like bones remember the body's shape long after,

what is made of earth holds the memory of the sky.

23.

What is moved by another

does not realize it is moving.

24.

When the first dawn came, it did not ask

for the night to end. So, the night does not ask

for the day to begin. Thus, the sky

teaches us the etiquette of dance.

25.

Fire does not want to exist

without darkness to hold it.

26.

Do not ask if animals can think or talk.

Can they suffer? [unreadable]

27.

Don't curse the darkness.

28.

Respect future people.

29.

The less you relax,

the luckier you will be.

30.

Energy in pursuit is the best test of willpower,

but it does not make the best hunter.

31.

Woman's spirit does not know law or justice,

to which man is enslaved [unreadable]…

she only yearns for the sea.

32..

The more complex the outside problem,

the deeper inside yourself you must go.

33.

The world can be changed

more by conversation

than by the worst storm.

34.

The space between the stars is not empty.

It is filled with the heartbeat of creation.

Listen.

35.

Breath is the common language of all life.

36.

Things never named

carry the naked truth.

37.

The wolf growls at us,

but never dares to question the moon.

38.

Before creation, there was the void.

After creation, there will be a void.

In the space between, the dance continues.

39.

You are not the body you wear [unreadable].

40.

Do, and you know.

41.

Over countless seasons,

the tallest mountains

earn a white crown.

42.

Millions of eggs a bug lays.

Only some hatch.

Yet bugs thrive.

43.

The red ants do not wait for a leader.

44.

Accumulating material wealth

is for those the tribe deems worthless.

45.

Men give as much as they take,

blood-drinkers[1] do not.

---

[1] Mosquitoes.

46.

Yesterday, it mattered how you knew.

Today, it matters what you know.

Tomorrow, it will matter who you know.

47.

Whatever you do to anyone,

you do to the mighty spirit.

48.

The waterfall might drown you

and the wildcat might eat you,

but whatever keeps you away

from the waterfall and the wildcat

is certain to destroy you.

49.

The hunter who only hunts for the kill is a fool.

The true hunt is the hunt for balance.

50.

In the chase, we learn the rhythm of life;

in the feast, we honor the rhythm of death.

51.

The earth whispers, the wise listen.

52.

Like the stone remembers

what the tree forgets,

the body remembers

what the mind forgets.

53.

The moon speaks in cycles,

not in haste.

54.

The quietest step

leaves the deepest mark.

55.

As the spirit gains strength,

the body loses it. Laughing.

56.

When there is no more I, me, mine,

there is [unreadable due to damage].

57.

Walk with the earth,

and you will never stray.

You will never stray.

58.

What is born in haste

is cursed with fragility.

Rushing leads to weakness.

Patience breeds strength.

59.

The fertile must serve the barren,

for the barren tend the roots.

60.

The action is not sacred,

the intention makes it so.

61.

The fire burns brightest
where we forbid it to spread.

62.

There is no shame in hunger,
but much shame in devouring
without gratitude.

63.

A woman's laugh is worth more
than a pile of skin and fur.

64.

The man who boasts of women

has not kept a single one.

65.

When the moon is full,

let no quarrels linger.

66.

A life spent chasing beauty

ends in an empty cave.

67.

The tribe that mocks its lovers

soon forgets how to laugh.

68.

Rhythm unites what words cannot.

The chant is older than the tongue.

69.

In the joining of bodies, the spirits dance.

Do not trample their rhythm

with thoughtless steps.

70.

Don't choke the stream; release it with care

and flood the valley with life.

71.

All creation begins in chaos;

wisdom guides it into form.

72.

As the child is not yours, but the tribe's…

the act is not yours, but belongs to the earth.

73.

Creation whispers its secrets loudest

in the silence after the storm,

to those who listen.

Listen.

74.

Do not waste fire. Use it to light others.

75.

When the moon speaks, the earth listens.

When the earth speaks, only men can hear.

Listen.

76.

Do not call the wolf wild.

The wolf calls the man wild.

77.

The moon did not need a name,

but men gave it one [unreadable due to damage].

78.

The sky holds no promise,

only the wings of they who dare.

79.

The earth never asks for rain [but]

always accepts it with care.

80.

The man who drinks from every stream

will die of thirst.

81.

The tree does not mourn the fall of leaves.

It sheds them to grow.

82.

You will be better if you hunt not for the catch

but for the knowing.

83.

The hunter's strength is in the knowing,

not the weapon.

84.

Do not wait to gather.

The light will not wait for you.

85.

If you are lost, do not run. Sit still,

and listen to the land.

86.

Happiness is found in desiring nothing,

not having it all.

87.

Wisdom never suggested

happiness is the goal.

88.

Who knows what is good?

They who know what is bad.

89.

The earth does not belong to you, you belong to it.

The earth does not belong to you, you belong to it.

The earth does not belong to you, you belong to it.

90.

Gather to share.

A full basket should be emptied.

91.

Everything will pass.

Take what is needed,

compost the rest.

92.

What you need will come

[unreadable due to damage].

93.

Never only look at what you see;

the formless spirit has no limit.

94.

What you need will come.

What you seek seeks you.

95.

Know well what you want, and lose sight of it

no more than the hawk loses sight of prey

96.

The thought comes before the thing.

Only man can think.

97.

The richest man is the one

able to give to others

more than he takes from them.

98.

Surrender to the desire for greatness[2].

99.

Just as you have a divine duty,

you have a divine diet.

---

[2] Big things; grandeur, idealism.

100.

Fiber binds the plant,

tendon binds the body,

duty binds the spirit.

101.

In the dark, the cave is home;

in the light, it is a tomb.

102.

When the wave realizes it is the ocean,

that [unreadable due to damage].

103.

[unreadable]

the trees will tell the birds

and the birds will tell the wind.

104.

To lie to a child is to break his leg.

105.

The needs of the many

do not outweigh the needs of the few;

every man has his own needs.

106.

The soil is the true wealth.

Without it, all will wither.

Without it, all will wither.

107.

The circle holds no head,

but all must hold its weight.

108.

The leader walks past when the meal is served

[unreadable due to damage].

109.

When men forget the circle

and seek to build towers,

they lose the songs of the earth.

110.

They fell not to beasts, nor aliens,

Nor black[3], nor hunger…

but to forgetting.

111.

The first to say 'I own'

will soon be the last to eat.

---

[3] Bacterial infection, presumably.

112.

When there is no heat left in the sun

[unreadable due to damage].

113.

There is beauty above

no shadow can touch.

114.

Do not ask the wind to change

[unreadable due to damage].

115.

The weight of words will never

be expressed in words.

116.

That which always and is…

what replenishes in measure

as it burns away.

117.

Do not eat your way toward sleep

like [unreadable due to damage].

118.

Courage is a convincing argument.

119.

Still, the wolf kills to eat…

not to hate.

120.

The tribe that cannot sit in silence

will fall to noise.

121.

Strike only to protect, never to prove.

122.

To harm is easy. To heal is power.

123.

A quiet mind hears the earth breathe.

Listen.

124.

The leader walks ahead to clear the path.

125.

Those who rule by fear fear the ruled.

126.

They bury their kings in mountains of stone,

but forget life.[4]

---

[4] This suggests they knew of a people who construct tombs for their kings. The Egyptians?

127.

A man who belongs to his people

will not belong to his king.

128.

The trees do not obey

[unreadable due to damage].

129.

They fill their belly with shiny metal

and die hungry.[5]

---

[5] This is acknowledgement of famine elsewhere (meaning they must
have seen a problem with large-scale monocultural food production.)
and a strong suggestion of metallurgy.

130.

Greatness is not found in stone.

Stone's existence is penance.

Soil is great. Listen.

131.

The hunter who wastes the kill

starves his children's children.

132.

May the tribe keep laughter forever.

133.

You are the forest, you are the wind,

[unreadable due to damage].

134.

Breath is borrowed, and returned, to the wind.

135.

A hunter who eats alone dies alone.

136.

Cannot read the irregular pulse of success.

137.

A full belly shared

feeds the heart twice.

138.

The weak man [among us]

is the measure of our strength.

139.

The stars are the tribe of the sky.

We are the stars of the earth.

140.

The grass-eaters[6] say

what is not seen

might not exist.

141.

The water sees your face,

but will not remember you.

------

[6] People who rely on grains, which are the harvested seeds of select grasses.

142.

To touch the sky you must let go of earth.

143.

The cut bleeds more from a kind hand.

144.

The man with the loudest voice must listen most.

145.

A leader eats last. The weak sleep hungry.

146.

They stack stones to honor men,

[and they] bury wisdom beneath.

147.

They who forget their tribe,

become their own enemy.

148.

When the wild ones saw our faces,

they laid down their spears.
They laid down their spears.

149.

When we arrived, the fire was already burning.

150.

The man who finds himself will find no enemy.

151.

To tame a river is to dry the land.

152.

No king's ashes will ever grow a leaf.

No king's tomb will ever reach the sky.

153.

To silence someone's song

is to wound the wind.

154.

Do not count time, count songs.

155.

No hunter ever owned the forest.

BROKEN, STILL SPEAKING

These fragments are not a puzzle to be solved, nor a story to be completed. They are a conversation interrupted by time, leaving us with the challenge—and the privilege—of listening across millennia.

What emerges is not certainty, but possibility; a priceless glimpse at the timeless.

These people wrote for the moment of discovery; for us; for now. Where we go from here is up to us.